Corporate Culture/ Operating System

Paramendra Bhagat

"If you think about business like a computer, culture is the operating system. Everything else is an "app." Finance is an app. Creative is an app. Strategy is an app. But culture is the operating system."
--- Gary Vaynerchuk.

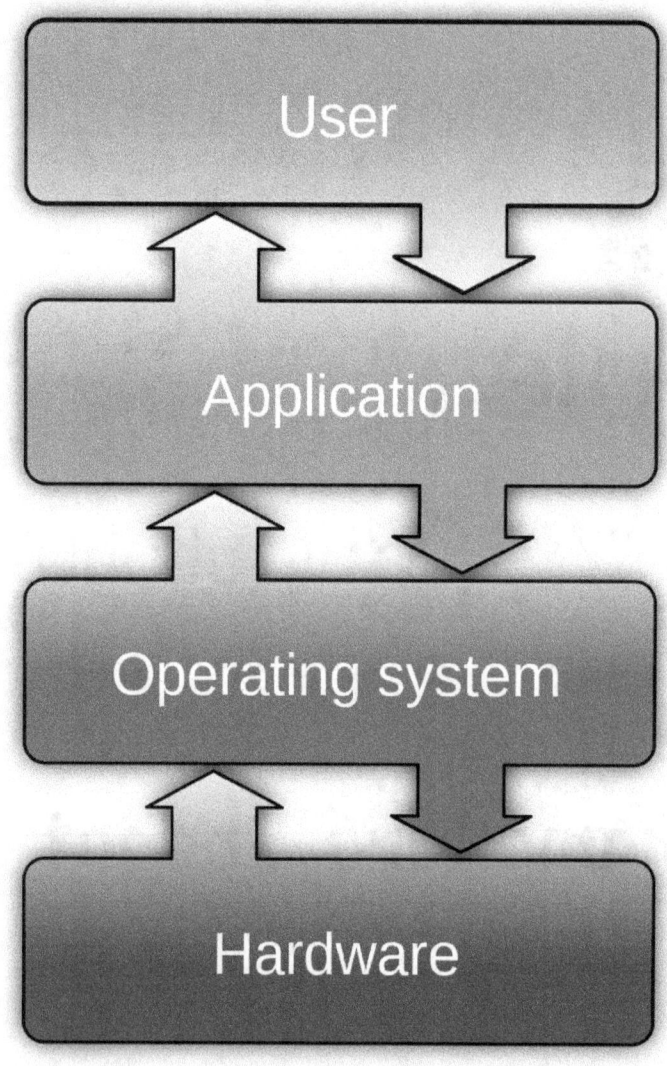

Dedicated to my father who owned the largest radio and electronics shop in my hometown Janakpurdham, Nepal, in his prime, and his grandfather, my great-grandfather, who started from scratch and ended up with the largest land-holding in our home village Gonarpura through hard work, thrift, foresight, and generosity.

Contents

Corporate Culture And Its Importance

Corporate culture refers to the shared values, beliefs, attitudes, and behaviors that characterize an organization. It is the way things are done in a company, including its customs, traditions, and unwritten rules. Corporate culture shapes the attitudes and behaviors of employees, affects their motivation, and influences their decisions.

Corporate culture is important because it can have a significant impact on the success of an organization. A strong and positive corporate culture can enhance employee morale, increase job satisfaction, and improve productivity. It can also help attract and retain top talent, as well as foster a sense of loyalty and commitment among employees.

On the other hand, a negative corporate culture can lead to high turnover, low morale, and poor performance. It can also create a toxic work environment that undermines the company's reputation and bottom line. Therefore, it is important for companies to cultivate a positive and supportive corporate culture that aligns with their values and goals.

The Six Core Components Of A Great Corporate Culture

At our company, we believe in a corporate culture that is built on six core values that guide our actions and behaviors:

1.   Work Hard: We are committed to working hard to achieve our goals and exceed expectations. We believe in putting in the time and effort needed to succeed, and we recognize and reward hard work.

2.   Play by the Rules: We believe in doing what is right, even when it's hard. We follow ethical principles and laws, and we hold ourselves to the highest standards of integrity and honesty. We do not tolerate theft, dishonesty, or unethical behavior.

3.   Innovate: We value creativity and innovation, and we encourage our employees to think outside the box. We are always looking for new and better ways to do things, and we embrace change as an opportunity to grow and improve.

4.	Treat People with Respect: We believe in treating all people with respect, regardless of their race, gender, age, or any other characteristic. We do not tolerate discrimination, harassment, or any other form of mistreatment. We strive to create a safe and inclusive work environment where everyone feels valued and supported.

5.	Communicate: We value open and honest communication, and we encourage our employees to speak up and share their ideas and concerns. We believe that effective communication is essential to building strong relationships and achieving our goals. We believe in open and honest communication, both within our team and with our clients and partners, to ensure transparency and accountability in all our interactions.

6.	Serve: We believe in great customer service. We also believe engaging in selfless service makes you better at customer service. We believe in giving back to our community and making a positive impact in the world. We encourage our employees to volunteer their time and talents to help others, and we support charitable organizations and causes that align with our values.

By embodying these values in everything we do, we are confident that we can create a corporate culture that fosters collaboration, innovation, and success for all.

Work Hard

At our company, we believe in the value of hard work. We recognize that success is not handed to us on a silver platter, but instead, it is the result of dedicated effort and perseverance. Therefore, we are committed to putting in the work needed to achieve our goals and strive for excellence in all that we do.

This commitment to hard work is evident in the way we approach our projects and tasks. We prioritize our work and focus on completing it to the best of our ability, without taking shortcuts or cutting corners. We understand that the quality of our work is a reflection of our company, and we take pride in delivering exceptional results that exceed expectations.

Moreover, we recognize that hard work is not limited to the individual level. We believe that a successful company is built on the collective effort of all its employees. Therefore, we encourage collaboration and teamwork to ensure that we are working towards a common goal. We believe that by sharing our knowledge and expertise, we can learn from each other and grow together.

We also recognize that hard work is not limited to the workday. We believe in putting in the extra effort to go above and beyond for our clients and community. Whether it is volunteering our time, contributing to charitable causes, or simply being there for someone in need, we believe that hard work extends beyond the boundaries of the workplace.

Ultimately, our commitment to hard work is a reflection of our dedication to excellence. We believe that by putting in the effort needed to achieve our goals, we can create a company culture that fosters success and growth. By embodying this value, we are confident that we can achieve great things, both individually and collectively.

(1)   The Greatest Rules For Personal Productivity

Personal productivity is the ability to use one's time and resources efficiently and effectively to achieve desired goals. In order to achieve optimal productivity, individuals need to develop habits and practices that help them to stay focused and motivated. Here are some of the greatest rules for personal productivity:

Set clear goals: Setting clear and specific goals helps to provide direction and focus. It helps individuals to prioritize their activities and allocate resources efficiently.

Prioritize: Prioritizing tasks is critical for effective time management. It involves identifying the most important tasks and focusing on them first.

Create a routine: Establishing a routine helps to create structure and consistency in daily activities. It helps to eliminate distractions and enables individuals to focus on their most important tasks.

Eliminate distractions: Distractions such as social media, phone calls, and email notifications can negatively impact productivity. To avoid these distractions, individuals should turn off notifications, set aside specific times for checking emails, and use tools like noise-canceling headphones to block out noise.

Take breaks: Taking regular breaks can help to boost productivity and prevent burnout. Short breaks of 5-10 minutes every hour can help to refresh the mind and prevent fatigue.

Use productivity tools: There are a variety of productivity tools available that can help individuals to manage their time more effectively. These tools can include calendars, to-do lists, and project management software.

Learn to say no: Saying no to tasks that are not aligned with one's goals and priorities can help to free up time and reduce stress.

Practice self-care: Taking care of one's physical and mental health is critical for productivity. Getting enough sleep, exercising regularly, and taking time for hobbies and interests can help individuals to feel more energized and focused.

Collaborate: Collaboration can help to generate new ideas and approaches to problem-solving.

Working with others can help to boost productivity and creativity.

Continuously improve: Continuously seeking to improve one's skills and knowledge can help individuals to stay competitive and achieve greater success. This involves setting aside time for learning and professional development activities.

(2)   Rules For Great Time Management

Here are some of the rules for great time management:

Set goals: It's essential to set clear goals for what you want to achieve. This will help you stay focused and motivated.

Prioritize tasks: Make a list of tasks and prioritize them based on their importance and urgency. Tackle the most critical tasks first.

Use a calendar: Use a calendar or planner to keep track of appointments, deadlines, and other important dates. This will help you stay organized and avoid missing important events.

Avoid multitasking: Multitasking can be counterproductive as it can reduce your productivity and increase stress levels. Instead, focus on one task at a time and give it your full attention.

Take breaks: It's essential to take regular breaks to avoid burnout and improve focus. Take short breaks every hour or so to recharge your batteries and increase productivity.

Eliminate distractions: Distractions can be a significant obstacle to productivity. Try to eliminate or minimize distractions such as social media, email notifications, and other interruptions.

Delegate tasks: If possible, delegate tasks to others to free up your time for more critical tasks. This will help you get more done in less time and reduce stress levels.

Learn to say no: Saying yes to every request can lead to overcommitment and burnout. Learn to say no to requests that are not essential or that you don't have time for.

Use technology to your advantage: There are many productivity apps and tools available that can help you manage your time more effectively. Experiment with different tools to find what works best for you.

Be flexible: Finally, it's essential to be flexible and adaptable. Things don't always go according to plan, so be prepared to adjust your schedule and priorities as needed.

(3)   The Importance Of Sleep And Rest To Productivity And Creativity

Sleep and rest are essential components of overall well-being and productivity. Adequate sleep and rest can improve brain function, increase focus and creativity, and reduce the risk of burnout and other negative health outcomes.

Studies have shown that lack of sleep can have a significant impact on cognitive performance, including attention, memory, and decision-making. Chronic sleep deprivation has also been linked to a higher risk of depression, anxiety, and other mental health issues.

Rest, including breaks during work hours and time off from work, is also crucial for maintaining productivity and creativity. Taking regular breaks throughout the workday can help reduce stress and prevent burnout. Additionally, time off from work, such as vacations or weekends, provides an opportunity to recharge and return to work with renewed energy and focus.

Research has also suggested that both sleep and rest play a critical role in promoting creativity. During sleep, the brain consolidates memories and processes information, which can help to spark new ideas and insights. Taking breaks and allowing the mind to rest can also facilitate creativity by allowing the brain to process information and generate new connections.

In contrast, pushing oneself to work for extended periods without adequate sleep or rest can lead to decreased productivity and creativity. Over time, this can result in burnout, a state of physical and emotional exhaustion that can impair cognitive function and lead to a range of negative health outcomes.

In summary, sleep and rest are essential components of personal productivity and creativity. Prioritizing these activities can lead to improved cognitive function, increased focus, and decreased risk of burnout and other negative health outcomes.

(4) The Importance Of Diet And Exercise To Being Productive

Maintaining a healthy diet and exercise routine is essential for being productive. A nutritious diet and regular exercise help keep the body and mind in top condition, allowing individuals to perform at their best. Here are some of the reasons why diet and exercise are important for productivity:

Improved Focus and Energy: Regular exercise helps improve blood circulation, delivering more oxygen and nutrients to the brain, which can improve cognitive function and help individuals focus better. Eating a healthy diet full of nutrient-rich foods, such as fruits, vegetables, and lean proteins, provides the body with the energy it needs to stay alert and focused throughout the day.

Reduced Stress: Exercise and a healthy diet have been shown to reduce stress levels. High levels of stress can negatively impact productivity, so finding ways to reduce stress is crucial. Exercise can help release endorphins, the body's natural "feel-good" chemicals, which can improve mood and help reduce stress levels. Additionally, eating a healthy diet that includes foods rich in vitamins and minerals can help reduce inflammation in the body, which can contribute to feelings of stress and anxiety.

Improved Physical Health: Regular exercise and a healthy diet help improve physical health. Physical health is essential for productivity because it allows individuals to perform daily tasks with ease and efficiency. Exercise can help build strength, increase flexibility and endurance, and reduce the risk of chronic diseases such as diabetes and heart disease. Eating a healthy diet can also help reduce the risk of chronic diseases and improve overall physical health.

Improved Mental Health: Exercise and a healthy diet have also been shown to improve mental health. Poor mental health can negatively impact productivity, so taking care of mental health is essential for being productive. Exercise can help improve mood and reduce symptoms of anxiety and depression. Eating a healthy diet can also improve mental health by providing the body with the nutrients it needs to function properly.

In summary, maintaining a healthy diet and exercise routine is crucial for being productive. Improved focus and energy, reduced stress, and improved physical and mental health are some of the benefits of following a healthy lifestyle.

(5) The Importance Of Family And Friends To Being Productive

When it comes to being productive, having a supportive network of family and friends can play an important role. Here are some reasons why:

Emotional support: Family and friends can provide emotional support, which can help you deal with stress and other challenges that may impact your productivity. Being able to talk to someone and get advice or encouragement can help you stay motivated and focused on your goals.

Accountability: Family and friends can help keep you accountable for your goals and tasks. If you share your plans with them, they can help you stay on track and remind you of your priorities.

Time management: Spending time with loved ones can help you manage your time better. It can motivate you to get your work done efficiently so that you have more time to spend with them.

Networking: Family and friends can also provide networking opportunities that can lead to new ideas or collaborations that could benefit your productivity.

Health and well-being: Strong relationships with family and friends have been linked to better health outcomes, including reduced stress levels and improved mental health. Taking care of your well-being can help you stay productive and creative.

In summary, family and friends can provide emotional support, accountability, time management skills, networking opportunities, and health benefits, all of which can contribute to increased productivity and creativity. It's important to prioritize these relationships in order to maintain a healthy work-life balance.

Play By The Rules

Play by the Rules: We operate with integrity and hold ourselves accountable to the highest standards of ethical conduct, following the 10 commandments and avoiding all forms of theft and dishonesty.

At our company, we believe in the importance of playing by the rules. We understand that the success of our organization is built on a foundation of trust and integrity, and we are committed to upholding these values in all of our actions and decisions.

To achieve this, we hold ourselves accountable to the highest standards of ethical conduct. We follow a strict code of ethics that guides our behavior and decision-making processes. We adhere to the 10 commandments and avoid all forms of theft and dishonesty. We understand that these values are not only essential for our success but are also critical to our reputation and credibility.

Operating with integrity means doing the right thing, even when it is not an easy thing. It means being honest and transparent in our dealings with our clients, partners, and colleagues. We believe that by holding ourselves accountable to these values, we can build a culture of trust and respect that benefits all those we work with.

Moreover, we recognize that playing by the rules is not just about following a set of guidelines. It is also about making ethical decisions in the face of difficult choices. It means being aware of the consequences of our actions and considering the impact they may have on others. It means being willing to speak up when we see something that is not in line with our values.

At our company, we take these values seriously, and we encourage all employees to uphold them in all their actions and decisions. We believe that by doing so, we can build a culture that fosters trust, respect, and accountability. We understand that playing by the rules is not always easy, but we believe that it is essential to our success and the success of our clients and partners.

(1) All Major Religious Traditions Support The Values Of The Ten Commandments

The Ten Commandments, also known as the Decalogue, are a set of biblical principles that have influenced morality and ethics across the globe. While the commandments are commonly associated with Judaism and Christianity, many of the principles can be found in other major religious traditions as well.

Here are some examples of how the values of the Ten Commandments are supported by other major religious traditions:

Islam: Islam has a set of moral principles called the Five Pillars of Islam. One of these pillars is Shahada, or the declaration of faith, which is similar to the commandment to have no other gods before God. The commandment to honor one's parents is also emphasized in Islamic teachings, as is the principle of not stealing or committing adultery.

Hinduism: Hinduism teaches the principle of ahimsa, or non-violence, which is similar to the commandment to not murder. The concept of dharma, or moral duty, emphasizes the importance of being truthful and not stealing. Additionally, the principle of aparigraha, or non-possessiveness, supports the commandment to not covet others' possessions.

Buddhism: Buddhism teaches the principle of the Eightfold Path, which includes the concept of right speech, similar to the commandment to not bear false witness. The principle of non-harming or non-violence is also emphasized, in line with the commandment to not murder.

Confucianism: Confucianism teaches the importance of respecting one's elders and ancestors, in line with the commandment to honor one's parents. The principle of ren, or benevolence, emphasizes the importance of treating others with kindness and respect, which supports the commandment to not bear false witness or commit adultery.

Sikhism: Sikhism emphasizes the importance of honesty, equality, and selfless service. These values align with several of the Ten Commandments, such as not bearing false witness, not coveting, and not stealing.

Overall, while the values of the Ten Commandments are commonly associated with Judaism and Christianity, many of these principles can be found in other major religious traditions as well. These universal principles serve as a foundation for ethical and moral behavior across cultures and religions.

Innovate

Innovate: We value creativity and innovation, and we encourage our employees to think outside the box. We are always looking for new and better ways to do things, and we embrace change as an opportunity to grow and improve.

Innovation is at the heart of our company. We believe that to stay competitive in today's fast-paced world, it is essential to be constantly adapting, growing, and improving. That's why we value creativity and innovation, and we encourage our employees to think outside the box and challenge the status quo.

We understand that innovation is not just about creating new products or services; it's about finding new and better ways to do things. It's about improving processes, enhancing customer experiences, and optimizing operations. We believe that by encouraging our employees to think creatively and embrace change, we can continue to push the boundaries of what's possible and stay ahead of the curve.

At our company, we believe in fostering a culture of innovation. We encourage our employees to share their ideas and insights openly and without fear of judgment. We recognize that the best ideas often come from unexpected places, and we are committed to creating an environment where everyone's contributions are valued and encouraged.

Moreover, we recognize that innovation requires risk-taking and a willingness to embrace failure. We understand that not every idea will be a success, but we believe that the process of trying and failing is an essential part of the innovation process. We encourage our employees to take calculated risks, learn from their failures, and use those lessons to continue to grow and improve.

Ultimately, we believe that innovation is essential to our success and the success of our clients and partners. By embracing change and challenging the status quo, we can continue to find new and better ways to meet the needs of our customers, improve our processes, and achieve our goals. We believe that by valuing creativity and innovation, we can continue to push the boundaries of what's possible and stay ahead of the curve.

(1)　Some Great Examples Of Innovation In Corporate History

There have been many great examples of innovation in corporate history, from game-changing inventions to revolutionary business models. Here are some of the greatest examples:

Apple: Apple has been a leader in innovation for decades, with products such as the iPod, iPhone, and iPad that have transformed the tech industry. The company's user-friendly design and focus on aesthetics have also been major drivers of its success.

Amazon: Amazon's innovative business model has disrupted traditional retail and changed the way we shop online. The company's use of customer data and its logistics capabilities have enabled it to offer fast and convenient delivery, while its expansion into new areas such as cloud computing has further diversified its offerings.

Ford: Henry Ford's introduction of the assembly line in the early 20th century revolutionized manufacturing and made cars more affordable for the average consumer. The company's innovations in mass production techniques have been studied and copied by other industries for decades.

Google: Google's search engine has transformed the way we find information online, while the company's expansion into areas such as online advertising, mobile devices, and artificial intelligence has continued to push the boundaries of innovation.

Tesla: Tesla's electric cars and focus on sustainable energy have disrupted the automotive industry and led to a shift away from fossil fuels. The company's innovations in battery technology and autonomous driving have also been major drivers of its success.

IBM: IBM has been a leader in innovation for over a century, with inventions such as the first mainframe computer and the floppy disk. The company's continued focus on research and development has also led to innovations in areas such as artificial intelligence and quantum computing.

Airbnb: Airbnb's innovative platform has disrupted the traditional hotel industry and allowed travelers to find unique and affordable accommodations around the world. The company's use of user-generated content and social media marketing has also been key to its success. In addition to disrupting the hotel industry, Airbnb has also expanded into the travel and tourism industry by offering experiences and activities that allow travelers to explore new places and connect with local cultures.

Microsoft: Microsoft's introduction of the Windows operating system in the 1980s transformed the computer industry and helped make personal computers accessible to a wider audience. The company's focus on software development has continued to drive innovation in areas such as productivity tools and cloud computing.

Netflix: Netflix's innovative business model has disrupted traditional media and entertainment industries by offering a subscription-based streaming service that allows users to watch TV shows and movies on demand. The company's use of data analytics to create personalized recommendations for users has also been a major driver of its success.

Intel: Intel's development of the microprocessor in the 1970s revolutionized the computer industry and enabled the creation of smaller and more powerful computers. The company's continued focus on research and development has also led to innovations in areas such as semiconductor manufacturing and artificial intelligence.

PayPal: PayPal's innovative online payment system has transformed the way we make transactions online, making it easier and more secure to send and receive money. The company's expansion into new areas such as mobile payments and digital wallets has further diversified its offerings.

SpaceX: SpaceX's focus on reusable rockets and space technology has disrupted the aerospace industry and helped make space exploration more accessible and affordable. The company's innovations in rocket design and propulsion systems have also pushed the boundaries of what is possible in space travel.

Procter & Gamble: Procter & Gamble's focus on consumer research and product innovation has led to the development of iconic brands such as Tide, Pampers, and Crest. The company's continued focus on sustainability and social responsibility has also been a major driver of its success.

These examples demonstrate how innovation can transform industries and create new opportunities for growth and success, while also improving the lives of people around the world.

(2)   Some Great Examples Of Business Process Innovation

Business process innovation involves improving the way a business operates, whether it's through the development of new technologies or the creation of new systems and processes. Here are some examples of companies that have successfully implemented business process innovation:

Toyota: The Toyota Production System, also known as Lean Manufacturing, revolutionized the way cars were produced. It is a system that eliminates waste, improves quality, and reduces production time.

McDonald's: The fast-food chain pioneered the use of assembly-line processes to speed up food preparation and service, making fast food even faster.

Amazon: Amazon's use of advanced algorithms and automation to manage its vast logistics and distribution network has helped the company to streamline its operations and deliver products faster and more efficiently.

Zara: Zara's business model is built on rapid prototyping, fast production, and just-in-time inventory management. The company can design, produce, and distribute new clothing lines to stores in just a few weeks.

FedEx: The company's use of barcoding and tracking technologies revolutionized the logistics industry and enabled customers to track their packages in real time.

Uber: The ride-sharing app created a new business model by connecting drivers with passengers via a mobile app, disrupting the traditional taxi industry.

Airbnb: The platform disrupted the hospitality industry by connecting homeowners with travelers seeking affordable accommodations, creating a new model of home-sharing and a new revenue stream for homeowners.

These examples demonstrate how innovation in business processes can lead to significant improvements in efficiency, quality, and customer experience, ultimately leading to increased profitability and growth.

Here are a few more examples of business process innovation:

Tesla: Tesla has disrupted the automotive industry by developing electric vehicles and an advanced charging network. Their production processes are also innovative, with a focus on automation and vertically integrated supply chains.

Google: Google's search algorithm revolutionized the way we find information online. Their use of big data and machine learning has also enabled them to develop innovative products such as Google Maps and Google Assistant.

Netflix: Netflix disrupted the entertainment industry by moving away from traditional cable and broadcast TV and creating a new business model based on streaming content. They use advanced algorithms to recommend content to users based on their viewing history.

IBM: IBM's development of the first mainframe computer in the 1960s revolutionized data processing and paved the way for modern computing. They also developed the first relational database management system, which is still widely used today.

Procter & Gamble: P&G has a long history of innovation, from the development of synthetic detergents in the 1940s to the creation of Swiffer in the 1990s. They use a stage-gate innovation process to develop new products and processes, which involves testing and refining ideas before bringing them to market.

Starbucks: Starbucks has revolutionized the coffee industry with its innovative store designs, high-quality coffee beans, and customer service. They have also developed advanced supply chain management systems to ensure the consistent quality of their products.

Here are some additional examples of business process innovation:

Apple: Apple's innovation in the design and manufacturing process of its products has enabled the company to create sleek, high-quality devices that have become iconic in the tech industry.

Tesla: Tesla's innovation in electric vehicle technology has disrupted the traditional automotive industry, while also implementing new business processes in areas such as direct-to-consumer sales and over-the-air software updates.

Google: Google's search algorithm and advertising platform revolutionized the way people find information online, while also creating new business processes around data analytics and digital marketing.

Walmart: Walmart's innovation in supply chain management and inventory control has enabled the company to keep costs low and provide customers with low-priced products, while also implementing new business processes in areas such as e-commerce and online grocery delivery.

Procter & Gamble: Procter & Gamble's innovation in consumer product development and marketing has enabled the company to create successful brands such as Tide, Pampers, and Crest, while also implementing new business processes in areas such as sustainability and corporate social responsibility.

IBM: IBM's innovation in computer technology and software development has enabled the company to create advanced business solutions such as artificial intelligence, cloud computing, and blockchain, while also implementing new business processes in areas such as agile development and remote work.

These examples show how business process innovation can come in many different forms, from product design and manufacturing to supply chain management and digital marketing. By implementing new technologies, processes, and strategies, companies can create competitive advantages that enable them to succeed in their respective industries.

(3)   Some Low-Tech Examples Of Innovation From India's Informal Sector

India's informal sector, which refers to unregistered and unregulated businesses and workers, has shown remarkable innovation in creating low-tech solutions to solve everyday problems. Here are some examples:

Chai Wallahs: Chai Wallahs are small tea stalls found all over India, often run by individuals who have limited resources and education. These chai wallahs have innovated by creating their own unique blends of tea and spices, as well as by developing low-cost ways of heating water and milk to make tea.

Street vendors: Street vendors in India have innovated by creating low-cost and portable food carts that enable them to sell their products on the go. These vendors have also developed creative packaging solutions that allow them to sell their products in small portions, which is especially important in a country where many people live on very low incomes.

Cycle rickshaws: Cycle rickshaws are a common mode of transportation in many Indian cities, especially for short distances. These rickshaws are often decorated and customized by their owners, and they have been modified with low-tech innovations such as custom seats, shade covers, and sound systems.

Barbers: In many Indian towns and cities, barbers operate in small, one-room shops or from makeshift outdoor stalls. These barbers have innovated by developing low-cost tools and techniques for hair cutting, such as using traditional straight razors and towels for shaving, rather than expensive electric shavers.

Traditional artisans: India has a rich tradition of handicrafts and artisanal goods, such as pottery, weaving, and embroidery. These artisans have innovated by developing new designs and products that appeal to modern tastes, while also preserving traditional techniques and materials.

These examples show that even in low-tech and informal settings, innovation can flourish. By developing creative solutions to everyday problems, these small business owners and workers have been able to create successful enterprises that provide valuable goods and services to their communities.

(4) Some Examples Of Jugaad.

Jugaad is a Hindi term that refers to a creative, improvised, and innovative solution to a problem using limited resources. It is a way of getting things done through quick and inventive means, often resulting in a cost-effective and efficient solution. Jugaad is commonly used in India's informal sector where resources and infrastructure are limited.

Here are some examples of jugaad:

Chotukool: A refrigerator created by Godrej using a thermoelectric cooling system instead of a compressor, making it more energy-efficient and affordable for rural areas.

Mitti Cool: A refrigerator made of clay that is capable of keeping vegetables and fruits fresh for several days without the need for electricity.

Sugarcane Juice Machine: A machine that is made from discarded bicycle parts, scrap metal, and a motor that can extract juice from sugarcane stalks.

Water Wheel: A device that is made from plastic drums and used to transport water from wells to homes in rural areas.

Stove for Ironing Clothes: A small stove made from an old paint can and a few other materials that are used to heat up irons for pressing clothes in small shops.

Chai Ka Tapri: A roadside tea stall that is made from a few bamboo sticks, a tarpaulin sheet, and some metal utensils.

These examples showcase the ingenuity and creativity of the informal sector in India, which often lacks access to advanced technology and resources.

(5) Examples Of Innovation From The Nonprofit Sector

The nonprofit sector has been responsible for many innovative solutions to address social, environmental, and economic challenges. Here are some examples of innovation from the nonprofit sector:

Microfinance: The Grameen Bank in Bangladesh was one of the first organizations to offer microfinance loans to people living in poverty, allowing them to start their own businesses and improve their lives.

Solar-powered lights: Nonprofits such as Liter of Light and SolarAid have developed affordable and sustainable solar-powered lights, providing access to electricity for people living in off-grid communities.

Clean water solutions: Organizations like Water.org and charity: water have developed innovative solutions to provide clean water to communities in need, including using low-cost water filtration systems and creating water kiosks.

Social impact bonds: Nonprofits such as Social Finance have pioneered the use of social impact bonds, a financial instrument that pays investors a return based on the social outcomes achieved, such as reducing recidivism rates or improving employment outcomes for disadvantaged youth.

Digital education tools: Nonprofits like Khan Academy have developed innovative digital education tools, providing free access to educational content for people around the world.

Community-led conservation: Nonprofits such as Rare have pioneered community-led conservation efforts, empowering local communities to protect their natural resources while also improving their livelihoods.

These are just a few examples of the many innovative solutions developed by nonprofits to address complex social and environmental challenges. Nonprofits often have a unique perspective and approach to problem

The nonprofit sector has been a driving force for innovation, particularly in the areas of social impact, community development, and environmental conservation. Here are some more examples of innovation from the nonprofit sector:

BRAC: BRAC, the world's largest NGO, has developed an innovative microfinance program that provides small loans to women in Bangladesh. The program has been replicated in other countries and has helped millions of women to start small businesses and improve their economic status.

Khan Academy: A nonprofit educational organization that offers free online courses and resources to students around the world. Khan Academy has revolutionized education by providing access to high-quality learning materials to anyone with an internet connection.

Charity: Water: A nonprofit organization that provides clean and safe drinking water to people in developing countries. Charity: Water has pioneered the use of technology to track its projects and communicate its impact to donors and supporters.

Teach for America: A nonprofit organization that recruits and trains recent college graduates to teach in underserved schools across the United States. Teach for America has had a significant impact on education reform by addressing the shortage of qualified teachers in low-income areas.

The Ocean Cleanup: A nonprofit organization that develops technology to remove plastic waste from the ocean. The Ocean Cleanup has developed an innovative system that uses passive floating barriers to collect plastic waste and prevent it from entering the ocean.

DonorsChoose: A nonprofit crowdfunding platform that connects teachers in need of classroom supplies with donors who want to support education. DonorsChoose has transformed the way teachers access resources and has helped to improve educational outcomes for students across the United States.

These examples demonstrate how nonprofits can drive innovation and create social impact through their work. By focusing on specific social or environmental problems, nonprofits can develop innovative solutions that can change lives and improve communities.

(6) Examples Of Innovation From The Public Sector From All Over The World And Various Time Periods In History

Here are some examples of innovation from the public sector across different time periods and locations:

Roman aqueducts: The Romans built a vast network of aqueducts to bring fresh water to their cities. This engineering marvel allowed for the growth and prosperity of Rome and other cities and served as a model for modern water systems.

Printing press: Johannes Gutenberg's invention of the printing press in the 15th century revolutionized the spread of information and led to the democratization of knowledge, making books and other printed materials more widely available.

Public education: In the 19th century, many countries began to establish public education systems that provided free schooling for all children. This innovation helped to increase literacy rates and provide greater opportunities for individuals from all backgrounds.

Green revolution: The green revolution in agriculture in the mid-20th century involved the use of advanced scientific techniques and new crop varieties to increase crop yields and combat hunger in developing countries.

Space exploration: The public sector has played a major role in space exploration, with NASA being the most prominent agency. Advances in space technology have led to many innovations, including satellite communications, GPS technology, and new materials.

E-government: Many governments have embraced technology to improve efficiency and transparency in government operations. This includes online services for things like tax filing, government procurement, and public information access.

Smart cities: With the growth of urbanization, many cities are implementing innovative technology to improve the quality of life for citizens. This includes things like smart transportation systems, energy-efficient buildings, and advanced data analytics to help cities make more informed decisions.

Universal healthcare: Many countries have implemented universal healthcare systems that provide access to healthcare for all citizens, regardless of their ability to pay. This has led to improved health outcomes and increased access to healthcare services.

Renewable energy: Many countries are investing in renewable energy sources like wind and solar power to reduce dependence on fossil fuels and combat climate change. This has led to many new innovations in renewable energy technology.

Digital government: Many governments are embracing digital technology to improve citizen engagement and increase efficiency in government operations. This includes things like online voting, crowdsourcing, and social media engagement.

These are just a few examples of innovation from the public sector across different time periods and locations.

(7) Some Top Breakthroughs In Science, Technology, And Business Upto The Year 2000

There have been numerous breakthroughs in science, technology, and business up to the year 2000 that have had a significant impact on our world. Here are some of the top breakthroughs in each field:

Science:

Discovery of DNA structure: In 1953, James Watson and Francis Crick discovered the structure of DNA, paving the way for the study of genetics and molecular biology.

Theory of relativity: In 1905, Albert Einstein published his theory of relativity, which revolutionized our understanding of space and time.

Penicillin: In 1928, Alexander Fleming discovered the antibiotic properties of penicillin, leading to the development of life-saving drugs.

Theory of evolution: In 1859, Charles Darwin published his theory of evolution, which explained the origin and diversity of species.

Atomic energy: In the 1940s, scientists developed the technology to harness the power of atomic energy, leading to the creation of nuclear power plants and weapons.

Technology:

Internet: In the 1960s, the development of packet-switching technology led to the creation of the internet, transforming the way we communicate and access information.

Personal computer: In the 1970s, the development of the personal computer brought computing power to the masses, revolutionizing the way we work and communicate.

Mobile phone: In the 1980s, the development of cellular technology led to the creation of the first mobile phones, transforming the way we communicate on the go.

GPS: In the 1970s, the US Department of Defense developed the Global Positioning System (GPS), which has revolutionized navigation and location-based services.

Airplane: In the early 20th century, the Wright brothers developed the first successful airplane, transforming the way we travel and connect with one another.

Business:

Ford Model T: In 1908, Henry Ford introduced the Model T, which made automobiles affordable for the average person and transformed transportation.

IBM PC: In 1981, IBM released its personal computer, which became the standard for business computing.

ATMs: In the 1960s, the first automated teller machines (ATMs) were introduced, revolutionizing the banking industry and making it easier for people to access their money.

Amazon.com: In 1995, Amazon.com was launched, introducing online shopping to the masses and transforming the retail industry.

Apple iPod: In 2001, Apple released the iPod, which revolutionized the music industry and transformed the way we listen to music.

(8) Some Major Breakthroughs In Science, Technology, And Business Since The Year 2000

Since the year 2000, there have been numerous breakthroughs in science, technology, and business that have had a significant impact on our world. Here are some of the top breakthroughs in each of these fields:

Science:

CRISPR gene-editing technology: Developed in 2012, this breakthrough technology allows scientists to easily and precisely manipulate DNA, opening up new possibilities for treating genetic diseases and improving crops.

Gravitational wave detection: In 2015, scientists were able to detect gravitational waves for the first time, confirming a major prediction of Einstein's theory of general relativity and opening up a new way to study the universe.

Human genome mapping: Completed in 2003, the Human Genome Project mapped the entire human genome, allowing scientists to better understand genetic diseases and develop new treatments.

Stem cell research: In recent years, scientists have made significant progress in developing stem cell therapies for a range of diseases, including cancer and heart disease.

Climate change research: Advances in climate change research have led to a better understanding of the impacts of human activity on the environment and helped to drive efforts to reduce greenhouse gas emissions.

Technology:

Smartphones: The introduction of the iPhone in 2007 revolutionized the way we communicate and access information, paving the way for a range of new technologies and services.

Cloud computing: Cloud computing has transformed the way businesses operate by providing a more flexible and cost-effective way to store and manage data.

Artificial intelligence: Rapid advances in AI technology have opened up new possibilities for everything from healthcare to autonomous vehicles.

Blockchain: Originally developed for the cryptocurrency Bitcoin, blockchain technology has the potential to transform a range of industries by enabling secure, decentralized transactions and record-keeping.

3D printing: 3D printing has made it possible to rapidly

There have been many groundbreaking breakthroughs in science, technology, and business since the year 2000. Here are some more examples:

Smartphones and Mobile Technology: The introduction of smartphones revolutionized the way we communicate, work, and interact with technology. With features such as internet access, GPS, cameras, and apps, smartphones have become an essential part of modern life.

Social Media: Social media platforms such as Facebook, Twitter, and Instagram have changed the way we connect with others, share information, and consume news.

Cloud Computing: Cloud computing allows users to store and access data and applications over the internet rather than on a local computer. This has increased accessibility and collaboration, particularly for remote teams.

Renewable Energy: The development and implementation of renewable energy sources such as solar and wind power have the potential to greatly reduce our dependence on fossil fuels and mitigate the effects of climate change.

CRISPR/Cas9 Genome Editing: CRISPR/Cas9 is a gene editing tool that allows for precise and efficient editing of DNA. This technology has the potential to revolutionize the fields of medicine, agriculture, and biotechnology.

Artificial Intelligence (AI): AI technologies such as machine learning, natural language processing, and robotics are transforming industries such as healthcare, finance, and manufacturing, and have the potential to greatly improve efficiency and productivity.

3D Printing: 3D printing technology has made it possible to create complex and customized objects with precision and speed. This has applications in fields such as manufacturing, medicine, and architecture.

Blockchain Technology: Blockchain is a decentralized digital ledger technology that allows for secure and transparent transactions without the need for intermediaries. This has potential applications in areas such as finance, supply chain management, and voting systems.

SpaceX and Commercial Spaceflight: The establishment of commercial spaceflight companies such as SpaceX has opened up new possibilities for space exploration and has the potential to greatly reduce the cost of space travel.

Sharing Economy: The sharing economy, which includes platforms such as Airbnb and Uber, has disrupted traditional industries such as hospitality and transportation and has enabled greater access to goods and services.

These breakthroughs have greatly impacted our world in the 21st century and will continue to shape the future.

(9) Some Of The Top Trends In Technology Going Forward

Artificial Intelligence: AI is expected to continue its growth in the coming years and will likely become even more sophisticated and integrated into our daily lives by 2030. This could include advancements in machine learning, natural language processing, and computer vision.

Internet of Things (IoT): With the increasing number of connected devices, the IoT is projected to grow significantly by 2030. Smart homes, smart cities, and other IoT applications could become even more prevalent.

Augmented and Virtual Reality (AR/VR): AR and VR technologies have already made significant advancements, and they are expected to continue to evolve by 2030. This could include improvements in the user experience, as well as new applications for these technologies in industries like healthcare, education, and entertainment.

Quantum Computing: Quantum computing is a nascent technology that could transform the way we process and store data. By 2030, quantum computing is projected to become more accessible and affordable, leading to significant breakthroughs in fields like cryptography, chemistry, and materials science.

Robotics: Robotics technology is expected to continue to grow and evolve by 2030, with advancements in fields like manufacturing, healthcare, and transportation. This could include new types of robots that are more advanced, capable of performing more tasks, and safer to operate around humans.

5G Networks: 5G technology is already being rolled out, and by 2030, it is projected to become even more widespread, leading to faster and more reliable internet connections, as well as new applications for this technology in fields like autonomous vehicles, smart cities, and healthcare.

These are just a few potential top trends in technology that could emerge by 2030, and there are sure to be many other breakthroughs and advancements that we can't even imagine yet.

(10) Some Of The Most Innovative Tech Entrepreneurs

It's difficult to pinpoint one single individual as the most innovative tech entrepreneur in human history, as there have been many influential figures who have contributed significantly to the field of technology. However, there are a few individuals who are often mentioned as some of the most innovative tech entrepreneurs based on their groundbreaking ideas, entrepreneurial spirit, and significant impact on the industry.

One of these individuals is Steve Jobs, the co-founder of Apple Inc. He is credited with revolutionizing the personal computer industry with the introduction of the Macintosh computer in 1984, and later with the iPod, iPhone, and iPad, which transformed the music and mobile phone industries. Jobs was known for his visionary approach to product design and marketing, as well as his ability to anticipate and create new markets.

Another influential tech entrepreneur is Bill Gates, the co-founder of Microsoft Corporation. Gates played a critical role in the development of the personal computer industry, and his company's Windows operating system became the dominant platform for personal computers. Gates is also known for his philanthropic work through the Bill and Melinda Gates Foundation, which focuses on improving global health and reducing poverty.

Elon Musk is another tech entrepreneur who is considered highly innovative for his work in various fields. He co-founded PayPal and later founded SpaceX, Tesla, Neuralink, and The Boring Company. His ventures have disrupted the financial, aerospace, automotive, and energy industries, and he is known for his ambitious vision of creating a sustainable future for humanity.

There are many other tech entrepreneurs who have made significant contributions to the field of technology, including Mark Zuckerberg (Facebook), Jeff Bezos (Amazon), Larry Page and Sergey Brin (Google), and many others. Ultimately, the title of the most innovative tech entrepreneur is subjective and can vary depending on personal opinions and criteria for innovation.

(11) Comparing Steve Jobs And Elon Musk In Terms Of Style

Steve Jobs and Elon Musk are two of the most iconic tech entrepreneurs of our time, each known for their unique approach to innovation and leadership. While both have achieved great success in their respective fields, their styles are quite distinct.

Steve Jobs was known for his design-focused approach, his obsessive attention to detail, and his tendency to control every aspect of the products he created. He was a visionary who could see the future of technology and was able to make it a reality through his relentless pursuit of perfection. He was a great storyteller who was able to convey his vision to his team and to the world, inspiring them to believe in his ideas and work tirelessly to bring them to life. He was also known for his sometimes abrasive personality and his tendency to be controlling, which sometimes caused conflict with his colleagues and partners.

On the other hand, Elon Musk is known for his engineering-focused approach, his willingness to take risks, and his ability to disrupt industries through his innovative ideas. He is a master of many disciplines, from engineering to physics to computer science, and he is able to bring these diverse fields together to create groundbreaking new technologies. He is also a great communicator, able to inspire his team and his followers with his grand vision for the future of humanity. However, he is also known for his impulsive behavior, his tendency to make bold promises that he sometimes can't keep, and his occasional clashes with regulators and the media.

Overall, while both Steve Jobs and Elon Musk are brilliant innovators who have made an indelible impact on the tech industry, their styles are quite different. Steve Jobs was a master of design and a great storyteller who was able to inspire his team to create beautiful and groundbreaking products, while Elon Musk is a master of engineering who is willing to take big risks to disrupt industries and bring his vision for the future to life.

(12) The Great Innovations Of Lee Kuan Yew, The Prime Minister of Singapore

Lee Kuan Yew, the founding father and first Prime Minister of Singapore, is known for his visionary leadership that transformed Singapore from a third-world country into a thriving, modern city-state. Here are some of his greatest innovations:

Housing Development Board (HDB): The HDB was established in 1960 to provide affordable public housing for the growing population of Singapore.

Under Lee's leadership, the HDB built more than one million public housing units, which now house more than 80% of Singapore's population.

Economic Development Board (EDB): The EDB was established in 1961 to attract foreign investment and promote economic growth in Singapore. Lee recognized the importance of foreign investment and worked to create a business-friendly environment that encouraged companies to invest in Singapore.

Port of Singapore: Lee recognized the importance of the port of Singapore as a key driver of economic growth. Under his leadership, the port was expanded and modernized, making it one of the busiest and most efficient ports in the world.

Cleanliness and Greenery: Lee believed that a clean and green environment was important for the well-being of Singaporeans and for attracting foreign investment. He launched a campaign to clean up the streets and public spaces and created a system of parks and green spaces throughout the city-state.

Education: Lee recognized that education was crucial to Singapore's success. He invested heavily in education, creating a system of high-quality schools and universities that has produced a highly skilled workforce and helped Singapore become a center of innovation and technology.

Multiculturalism: Singapore is a diverse country with a mix of ethnicities and cultures. Lee recognized the importance of fostering harmony and respect among different groups and worked to promote multiculturalism and tolerance in Singaporean society.

Overall, Lee Kuan Yew's greatest innovation was his vision for Singapore as a modern, prosperous, and well-governed city-state. His policies and leadership transformed Singapore into a thriving economic and cultural hub, setting an example for other developing countries around the world.

(13) Comparing Fire And The Wheel To Modern Technology Breakthroughs

Fire and the wheel are considered two of the most important innovations in human history, as they revolutionized the way people lived and interacted with their environment. In the same way, modern technology breakthroughs have significantly changed the way we live and work.

Fire allowed early humans to cook their food, stay warm during cold weather, and provide light in the darkness. Today, we have a wide range of technologies that have revolutionized the way we use fire, including electric and gas stoves, ovens, and heaters. These innovations have made cooking and heating much more efficient, safe, and convenient.

The wheel allowed humans to transport goods and people over long distances, making trade and travel much more manageable. Today, we have a vast array of transportation technologies, including cars, trains, planes, and ships, which have significantly reduced travel times and made it possible to transport people and goods quickly and efficiently.

Similarly, modern technology has brought about innovations that have significantly impacted our lives. For example, the internet has transformed the way we communicate, access information, and conduct business. Smartphones and mobile devices have made it possible for us to stay connected with others and access information on the go. Artificial intelligence and machine learning technologies are enabling us to automate many tasks and make more informed decisions based on data analysis.

In conclusion, while fire and the wheel were groundbreaking innovations in their time, modern technology breakthroughs have taken human innovation to new heights, transforming the way we live, work, and interact with our environment.

Treat People With Respect

Treat People with Respect: We believe in treating all people with respect, regardless of their race, gender, age, or any other characteristic. We do not tolerate discrimination, harassment, or any other form of mistreatment. We strive to create a safe and inclusive work environment where everyone feels valued and supported.

At our company, we believe that treating people with respect is essential. We understand that our success is built on the contributions of our employees, clients, and partners, and we are committed to creating a safe and inclusive work environment where everyone feels valued and supported.

We believe that respecting all people, regardless of their race, gender, age, or any other characteristic, is not only the right thing to do but is also critical to our success. We understand that when people feel respected and supported, they are more likely to be engaged and productive in their work. Moreover, we recognize that a diverse and inclusive workforce is essential to our success and the success of our clients and partners.

To achieve this, we do not tolerate discrimination, harassment, or any other form of mistreatment. We hold ourselves accountable to the highest standards of ethical conduct, and we expect the same from our employees, clients, and partners. We strive to create a culture of respect and inclusion where everyone feels comfortable expressing themselves and their ideas openly and without fear of judgment.

We understand that creating a safe and inclusive work environment is an ongoing process that requires constant attention and effort. We are committed to providing ongoing training and education to our employees to promote diversity, equity, and inclusion in all aspects of our business. We believe that by valuing and respecting all people, we can continue to attract and retain the best talent, build strong relationships with our clients and partners, and achieve our goals.

Ultimately, we believe that treating people with respect is not only the right thing to do, but it is also critical to our success as an organization. We are committed to creating a culture where everyone feels valued and supported, and where diversity and inclusion are celebrated. We believe that by doing so, we can continue to achieve great things and make a positive impact in the world.

(1) The Most Important Elements Of Building A Team

Building a successful team is a critical task for any organization, and it requires attention to several important elements. Here are some of the most essential elements of building a team:

Clear Goals: A team must have a clear understanding of the goals it is trying to achieve. This means that the team's goals should be well-defined, measurable, and realistic. The team should be aware of the resources it has to achieve the goals, the time frame in which the goals should be achieved, and the expected outcomes.

Roles and Responsibilities: Each member of the team should have a clear understanding of their role and responsibilities within the team. This helps to prevent misunderstandings and confusion and ensures that everyone is working towards the same goals.

Communication: Communication is key to building a successful team. The team should have open and clear communication channels, and team members should feel comfortable sharing their ideas and concerns. Regular meetings should be held to discuss progress, identify issues, and plan the next steps.

Trust: Trust is critical to the success of any team. Each team member should trust their colleagues to do their jobs, meet their commitments, and communicate openly and honestly. Team members should feel that they can rely on each other to achieve their shared goals.

Diversity: A team that is diverse in terms of skills, experience, and perspectives is more likely to be successful. This diversity can lead to more creativity and innovation and can help the team to identify and solve problems more effectively.

Recognition and Support: It is essential to recognize and support the contributions of each team member. This can help to build morale, encourage teamwork, and ensure that everyone feels valued and appreciated.

By focusing on these elements, teams can work together more effectively to achieve their goals and deliver successful outcomes.

(2) Top Team Building Exercises Used By Corporations

Team building exercises are an effective way to promote collaboration, communication, and trust among team members. Here are some of the top team-building exercises used by corporations:

Scavenger Hunt: This classic team-building exercise is a great way to promote teamwork and problem-solving skills. Teams are given a list of clues and have to work together to find the items on the list.

Trust Fall: This exercise involves one team member standing on a platform and falling backward, trusting their team members to catch them. This helps build trust and communication skills.

Escape Room: This popular team-building exercise involves a group of people working together to solve puzzles and escape from a locked room. It promotes problem-solving skills, communication, and teamwork.

Blindfolded Obstacle Course: This exercise involves one team member being blindfolded and guided through an obstacle course by their team members. This promotes trust, communication, and leadership skills.

Improv Games: Improv games such as "Yes, and" and "Storytelling" are fun ways to build teamwork and communication skills.

Outdoor Adventure Activities: Activities such as rock climbing, zip-lining, and hiking promote teamwork, communication, and trust.

Volunteer Work: Participating in volunteer work as a team is a great way to build teamwork and promote a sense of community.

Overall, team-building exercises are an effective way to promote collaboration, communication, and trust among team members.

(3) How To Confront Sexism In A Corporate Setting?

Confronting sexism in a corporate setting can be challenging, but it is important to create a workplace culture that is respectful and inclusive of all employees. Here are some steps that can be taken to address sexism in the workplace:

Educate yourself and your team: Educate yourself and your colleagues on what constitutes sexism and how it can impact individuals and the workplace as a whole. Provide training and workshops that address gender equality, unconscious bias, and how to create an inclusive workplace culture.

Address sexist behavior immediately: If you observe or experience sexist behavior, it's important to address it immediately. This can be done by speaking directly to the person who exhibited the behavior, or by reporting it to a manager or HR representative.

Create policies and procedures: Implement policies and procedures that clearly outline the consequences of engaging in sexist behavior. This can include disciplinary action and termination for repeat offenders.

Foster an inclusive environment: Create an environment where all employees feel valued and included, regardless of gender or any other characteristic. Encourage open communication and feedback, and actively work to eliminate any barriers to inclusivity.

Lead by example: As a leader, it's important to model inclusive behavior and hold yourself accountable for creating a workplace culture that is respectful and supportive of all employees.

Overall, confronting sexism in a corporate setting requires a proactive approach, clear policies and procedures, and a commitment to creating a workplace culture that is inclusive and respectful of all individuals.

(4) How To Confront Racism In A Corporate Setting?

Confronting racism in a corporate setting can be challenging, but it is important to address it to create a more inclusive and diverse workplace. Here are some steps you can take to confront racism in the workplace:

Educate yourself: Learn about the different types of racism, including unconscious bias, microaggressions, and systemic racism. Understanding the nuances of racism will help you better identify and address it.

Speak up: If you witness racist behavior, don't stay silent. Speak up and let the person know that their behavior is not acceptable. This can be done in a private conversation or in a group setting, depending on the situation.

Report incidents: If you experience or witness racism, report it to HR or another designated person in your company. Provide as much detail as possible, including the date, time, location, and people involved. Your company should have a clear process for reporting and addressing incidents of discrimination.

Support your colleagues: If someone has experienced racism, offer your support and be an ally. Listen to their experiences, acknowledge their feelings, and work together to create a more inclusive workplace.

Hold people accountable: Make sure that racist behavior is not tolerated in your workplace. Hold people accountable for their actions and ensure that there are consequences for discriminatory behavior.

Continue the conversation: Confronting racism is an ongoing process. Continue to have open and honest conversations about race and diversity in your workplace. This will help to create a culture of inclusivity and respect.

Confronting racism in the workplace can be uncomfortable, but it is necessary to create a more equitable and just workplace. By taking these steps, you can help to create a workplace where everyone feels valued and respected.

(5) How Best To Build A Remote Team?

As remote work becomes more common, building a remote team has become an essential part of many businesses. Building and managing a remote team presents unique challenges, but with the right strategies and tools, it can be just as effective as working in an office. Here are some best practices for building a successful remote team:

Hire the right people: When building a remote team, it's important to find people who are self-motivated, organized, and able to work independently. Look for candidates who have experience working remotely or who have the skills to do so successfully.

Communicate regularly: Communication is key to building a successful remote team. Make sure to have regular team meetings, and one-on-one meetings with each team member, and use messaging apps like Slack or Microsoft Teams to stay in touch throughout the day.

Establish clear expectations: Be clear about your expectations for your remote team. Set goals, and deadlines, and make sure everyone knows what they need to do to meet them.

Use technology: Remote teams rely on technology to stay connected and collaborate. Use project management tools like Trello or Asana, video conferencing tools like Zoom or Google Meet, and messaging apps like Slack or Microsoft Teams to stay in touch and work together.

Encourage collaboration: Just because your team is remote doesn't mean they can't collaborate. Encourage team members to work together on projects, share ideas and feedback, and collaborate on problem-solving.

Build a strong company culture: Building a strong company culture is especially important for remote teams. Encourage team members to participate in virtual team-building activities, celebrate successes together, and create a sense of community.

Provide the right resources: Make sure your remote team has the resources they need to be successful. This includes access to the right technology, tools, and training.

By following these best practices, you can build a successful and productive remote team.

Communicate

Effective communication is the foundation of success in any organization, and we believe that this is particularly true in our company. We prioritize openness and honesty because we understand that these are crucial to building trust with our employees, clients, and partners. By creating an environment where everyone feels comfortable sharing their ideas and concerns, we foster a culture of collaboration, innovation, and creativity.

We also recognize that communication is a two-way process that involves active listening and empathetic responses. It is not enough to simply speak our minds; we must also be willing to listen to others and take their perspectives into account. This means actively seeking out feedback and engaging in constructive dialogue to build stronger relationships with our stakeholders.

Clear and concise communication is critical to avoiding misunderstandings and conflicts. We strive to provide easily understandable information to our stakeholders through various communication channels. Meetings, emails, and social media are just a few examples of the channels we use to ensure that information is communicated effectively and efficiently.

Transparency and accountability are also essential components of effective communication. We keep our stakeholders informed about our progress, successes, and failures so that everyone is on the same page. This creates an environment of trust and credibility, which is essential to building strong relationships.

We also value diversity of thought and perspective, recognizing that everyone brings unique experiences and insights to the table. By seeking out feedback and actively engaging in dialogue, we can continuously improve our communication and work processes.

To ensure that our employees have the necessary skills to communicate effectively, we provide regular training and feedback. This includes training on active listening, conflict resolution, and effective communication in different contexts, such as in meetings or written communication.

By promoting open communication and creating an environment of trust and credibility, we can build stronger relationships with our stakeholders, including employees, clients, and partners. Ultimately, we believe that by prioritizing communication and seeking to continuously improve, we can make a positive impact in the world and achieve our organizational goals.

(1) The Top Rules Of Great Communication

There are several rules that can help to improve communication and make it more effective. Here are some of the top rules of great communication:

Be clear and concise: Use simple and straightforward language to convey your message. Avoid using jargon or complicated terms that your audience may not understand.

Listen actively: Pay attention to what the other person is saying and try to understand their perspective. Don't interrupt or talk over them.

Be empathetic: Try to see things from the other person's point of view and show that you understand their feelings and concerns.

Be respectful: Treat others with respect and courtesy, even if you disagree with them. Avoid using aggressive or confrontational language.

Be open-minded: Be willing to consider different ideas and perspectives. Don't be afraid to admit when you're wrong or when you don't know something.

Use nonverbal cues: Pay attention to your body language and tone of voice. Use gestures and facial expressions to convey your message and show interest in what the other person is saying.

Be aware of cultural differences: Communication styles and norms can vary across cultures, so it's important to be aware of these differences and adjust your communication style accordingly.

Follow up: After a conversation, follow up with the other person to ensure that you both understand each other's perspectives and that any issues have been addressed.

By following these rules, you can improve your communication skills and build stronger relationships with others.

(2) The Top Rules Of Assertive Communication

Assertive communication is a communication style that involves expressing yourself clearly, confidently, and respectfully while also respecting the rights and feelings of others. Here are some top rules of assertive communication:

Use "I" statements: Use "I" statements to express how you feel, what you need, or what you want. This makes it clear that you are expressing your own thoughts and feelings, rather than blaming or criticizing others.

Be specific: When making requests or expressing concerns, be specific about what you want or need. This helps to avoid misunderstandings and ensures that your message is clear.

Stay calm: Maintain a calm and composed demeanor when expressing yourself, even in difficult or stressful situations. This helps to convey confidence and respect for others.

Use confident body language: Use confident body language, such as maintaining eye contact and speaking in a clear and assertive tone, to convey confidence and assertiveness.

Practice active listening: When someone else is speaking, practice active listening by giving them your full attention and reflecting back on what you've heard to ensure that you understand their perspective.

Be respectful: Show respect for the other person's feelings and needs, even if you don't agree with them. Avoid using aggressive or confrontational language.

Set boundaries: Be clear about your boundaries and communicate them respectfully. This helps to ensure that your needs are respected and that you are not taken advantage of.

By following these rules, you can communicate assertively and effectively while also respecting the rights and feelings of others.

(3)   The Top Rules For Respectful Communication

Respectful communication involves expressing yourself in a way that shows consideration and regard for the feelings, needs, and rights of others. Here are some top rules for respectful communication:

Listen actively: Pay attention to what the other person is saying, without interrupting or dismissing their ideas. Try to understand their perspective and show empathy.

Speak respectfully: Use a respectful and considerate tone when speaking to others. Avoid using aggressive, rude, or derogatory language.

Avoid assumptions: Avoid making assumptions about what the other person is thinking or feeling. Instead, ask questions to clarify their perspective.

Be open-minded: Be willing to consider other viewpoints and opinions, even if they differ from your own. Be open to new ideas and perspectives.

Show appreciation: Acknowledge the contributions and efforts of others, and express gratitude for their help or support.

Apologize when necessary: If you have said or done something that has hurt or offended someone, apologize and take responsibility for your actions.

Use nonverbal cues: Pay attention to your nonverbal cues, such as facial expressions and body language. Use these cues to convey respect and interest in what the other person is saying.

Focus on solutions: When discussing problems or conflicts, focus on finding solutions that are respectful and considerate of everyone's needs.

By following these rules, you can communicate in a way that is respectful and considerate of others, which can help to build stronger and more positive relationships.

(4) How To Confront A Bully In A Corporate Environment?

Confronting a bully in a corporate environment can be challenging, but it is important to take steps to address the situation and protect yourself. Here are some tips on how to confront a bully in a corporate environment:

Keep records: Keep a record of any incidents of bullying, including the date, time, location, and what was said or done. This can help you to build a case and provide evidence if necessary.

Remain calm and professional: When confronting a bully, it's important to remain calm and professional. Avoid becoming emotional or defensive, as this can escalate the situation.

Be assertive: Be clear and assertive in your communication with the bully. State your concerns and expectations in a calm and confident manner.

Use "I" statements: Use "I" statements to express how you feel about the situation, rather than blaming or accusing the bully. For example, say "I feel uncomfortable when you speak to me in that tone of voice" rather than "You are being disrespectful."

Seek support: Talk to a trusted colleague, supervisor, or HR representative about the situation. They can provide support and guidance on how to address the issue.

Consider mediation: If the situation is not improving, consider mediation to help facilitate a constructive conversation between you and the bully. This can help to find a mutually acceptable solution.

Take action: If the bullying persists, consider filing a complaint with HR or speaking to a lawyer about legal options.

Remember, confronting a bully in a corporate environment can be difficult, but it is important to take steps to protect yourself and create a safe and respectful workplace environment.

(5) When In-Person Communication Is Better

While electronic communication such as emails, instant messaging, and video calls have become ubiquitous in today's fast-paced world, there are certain circumstances where in-person communication is best or better. Here are some examples:

Delivering bad news: When delivering bad news such as the loss of a job, a diagnosis of a serious illness, or the death of a loved one, in-person communication is usually the most appropriate and compassionate approach.

Negotiating: When negotiating with clients, partners, or vendors, in-person communication allows you to read nonverbal cues and build a stronger rapport and trust.

Team building: When building a team or fostering team cohesion, in-person communication can be more effective in creating a sense of community and shared purpose.

Brainstorming: When generating new ideas or solving complex problems, in-person communication can facilitate more dynamic and spontaneous exchanges of ideas.

Training and development: When providing training or coaching to employees, in-person communication can be more effective in providing hands-on experience and feedback.

Building relationships: When building and maintaining relationships with colleagues, clients, or partners, in-person communication allows for a deeper connection and better understanding of each other's needs and perspectives.

In summary, in-person communication is best suited for situations that require empathy, nuance, and a personal touch, while electronic communication is better for quick, efficient exchanges of information.

(6) Top Methods For Active Listening

Active listening is a critical skill for effective communication and involves giving your full attention to the speaker, understanding their message, and responding appropriately. Here are some top methods for active listening:

Give your full attention: Focus on the speaker and avoid distractions such as electronic devices or interruptions. Maintain eye contact and use nonverbal cues such as nodding to show that you are engaged and listening.

Avoid interrupting: Allow the speaker to finish their thoughts without interrupting or finishing their sentences. This demonstrates respect and shows that you are truly listening.

Ask questions: Ask open-ended questions to clarify the speaker's message and show interest in what they are saying. Paraphrase or repeat back what you heard to ensure you understand correctly.

Summarize: After the speaker has finished, summarize the key points to demonstrate that you have understood their message. This can also help to identify any misunderstandings or miscommunications.

Show empathy: Acknowledge the speaker's feelings and show that you understand their perspective. Use phrases such as "I can see how that would be difficult" or "I understand how you feel."

Avoid judgment: Avoid making judgments or assumptions about the speaker's message or motives. Listen without bias and keep an open mind.

Respond appropriately: Respond in a way that is appropriate and respectful, based on the speaker's message and needs. This could involve providing feedback, advice, or simply showing support and empathy.

By using these methods for active listening, you can improve your communication skills and build stronger relationships based on mutual understanding and respect.

Serve

Serve: We believe in giving back to our community and making a positive impact in the world. We encourage our employees to volunteer their time and talents to help others, and we support charitable organizations and causes that align with our values.

Corporate social responsibility has become an essential aspect of modern-day business. At our company, we understand the importance of giving back to our community and making a positive impact in the world. Our core value of "Serve" reflects our commitment to being responsible corporate citizens and using our resources to create positive change in the world.

We recognize that we have a responsibility to support charitable organizations and causes that align with our values. We believe that by supporting these organizations, we can make a meaningful difference in the lives of those who need it most. We encourage our employees to volunteer their time and talents to these organizations, and we provide them with opportunities to do so. We believe that by giving back to our community, we can build stronger relationships with our employees, clients, and partners, and create a more engaged and motivated workforce.

Moreover, we believe that serving our community is not just about giving back, but it is also about building stronger relationships with our clients and partners. We understand that many of our clients and partners also value community service, and by working together on charitable projects, we can build stronger bonds and achieve greater impact.

We are committed to being responsible corporate citizens, and we support organizations that promote social and environmental sustainability. We believe that sustainability is a critical issue facing our world today, and we are committed to doing our part to address it. We strive to minimize our environmental impact, promote ethical business practices, and invest in the well-being of our employees and the communities in which we operate.

We believe that by serving our community and supporting charitable organizations, we can make a positive impact in the world and build a better future for everyone. We are committed to making a difference in the world, and we invite our employees, clients, and partners to join us in this important work.

(1) Some Great Examples Of Customer Service

There have been many examples of exceptional customer service in corporate history that have helped companies build strong reputations and loyal customer bases. Here are a few notable examples:

Zappos: Zappos is often cited as a prime example of outstanding customer service. The online shoe and clothing retailer has built its entire business around the concept of providing exceptional customer experiences. Zappos is known for its fast and free shipping, easy returns, and 24/7 customer service. They even offer a 365-day return policy and encourage their employees to go above and beyond to make customers happy.

Nordstrom: Nordstrom has a reputation for providing exceptional customer service that goes above and beyond what is expected. The upscale department store is known for its liberal return policy, which allows customers to return items without a receipt and even if the item was not purchased at Nordstrom. They also have a legendary policy of empowering their sales staff to do whatever it takes to make their customers happy.

Amazon: Amazon is known for its customer-centric approach to business. The online retailer has a reputation for providing fast and reliable shipping, easy returns, and outstanding customer service. They have invested heavily in technology to make it easy for customers to find what they are looking for and to make the purchasing process as smooth as possible.

Ritz-Carlton: The Ritz-Carlton hotel chain is renowned for its exceptional customer service. The luxury hotel brand has a motto of "We are Ladies and Gentlemen serving Ladies and Gentlemen" and has a reputation for anticipating the needs of their guests and going above and beyond to make their stay memorable. They empower their employees to make decisions that will delight their guests and create a personalized experience for each guest.

Disney: Disney is known for its magical customer experiences. From the moment guests enter one of their theme parks, they are immersed in a world of fantasy and adventure. Disney's employees, or "cast members," are trained to be friendly and helpful and to create memorable experiences for their guests. Disney has a reputation for going above and beyond to make guests' dreams come true.

These companies and many others have set the bar high for exceptional customer service, and they serve as an inspiration for other companies to prioritize the customer experience and build strong, lasting relationships with their customers.

(2) Some Great Examples Of Selfless Service

Selfless service, or acts of kindness and sacrifice done without expectation of reward or recognition, have been demonstrated by many individuals throughout human history. Here are some examples of some of the greatest examples of selfless service:

Mother Teresa: Mother Teresa was a Catholic nun who dedicated her life to helping the poor and sick in India. She founded the Missionaries of Charity, which has provided care and support to people in need around the world. Mother Teresa received numerous honors for her humanitarian work, including the Nobel Peace Prize.

Mahatma Gandhi: Mahatma Gandhi was an Indian political leader and social activist who is known for his philosophy of nonviolent resistance. He led India to independence from British rule through peaceful protests and civil disobedience, inspiring similar movements around the world.

Florence Nightingale: Florence Nightingale was a British nurse and social reformer who is credited with founding modern nursing. She worked tirelessly to improve the conditions of hospitals and care for the sick and wounded during the Crimean War. Her efforts led to the development of better sanitation practices and medical care.

Martin Luther King Jr.: Martin Luther King Jr. was an American civil rights leader who fought against racial discrimination and segregation in the United States. He advocated for nonviolent resistance and peaceful protest, leading the famous March on Washington and delivering his iconic "I Have a Dream" speech.

Oskar Schindler: Oskar Schindler was a German industrialist who is credited with saving the lives of over 1,000 Jewish people during the Holocaust. He employed them in his factories and provided them with food and protection, risking his own life in the process.

Abdul Sattar Edhi: Abdul Sattar Edhi was a Pakistani philanthropist who founded the Edhi Foundation, a nonprofit organization that provides free healthcare, education, and social services to people in need in Pakistan. He received numerous awards for his humanitarian work, including the Gandhi Peace Prize and the Ramon Magsaysay Award.

Wangari Maathai: Wangari Maathai was a Kenyan environmental activist and Nobel Peace Prize laureate who founded the Green Belt Movement, an organization that promotes environmental conservation and community development through tree planting and education.

These are just a few examples of the many individuals who have demonstrated selfless service throughout history. Their actions have inspired others to follow in their footsteps and make a positive impact on the world.

(3)   Some Ways To Volunteer To Do Service Work Over A Weekend

There are many great ways to volunteer and do service work over a weekend. Here are a few ideas:

Habitat for Humanity: Habitat for Humanity is a nonprofit organization that builds affordable housing for families in need. They often have weekend volunteer opportunities for individuals or groups to help with construction or other tasks.

Animal Shelters: Local animal shelters are often in need of volunteers to help with tasks such as walking dogs, cleaning cages, and socializing with animals. Spend a weekend volunteering at an animal shelter to help make a difference in the lives of these furry friends.

Food Banks: Food banks provide food and other essentials to people in need. Spend a weekend volunteering at a local food bank, sorting donations, and packing food boxes for distribution.

Environmental Cleanups: Volunteer for an environmental cleanup event in your community. Help to clean up local parks, beaches, or other areas that need attention.

Community Gardens: Many communities have gardens that are maintained by volunteers. Spend a weekend volunteering in a community garden, helping to plant and harvest fresh produce for local residents.

Elderly Care: Volunteer at a local nursing home or senior center, spending time with elderly residents and assisting with activities such as games, crafts, or exercise classes.

Youth Mentoring: Volunteer with a youth mentoring program, such as Big Brothers Big Sisters, to make a positive impact on the life of a child. Spend a weekend engaging in activities and building a relationship with a young person in need of a mentor.

These are just a few examples of the many ways you can volunteer and do service work over a weekend. Whatever your interests or passions may be, there is likely a volunteer opportunity that aligns with them and provides a meaningful way to give back to your community.

(4) How Engaging In Volunteer Service Work Makes You Better At Customer Service

Engaging in volunteer service work can provide valuable experiences and skills that can make you better at customer service. Here are some ways volunteering can improve your customer service skills:

Communication skills: Volunteering often involves working with people from diverse backgrounds and experiences. This can improve your ability to communicate effectively with a variety of customers, even those who are difficult to understand or work with.

Empathy and understanding: Volunteering can help you develop a deeper sense of empathy and understanding toward others. This can be particularly helpful in customer service, where you may encounter customers who are frustrated or upset. By empathizing with their situation and trying to understand their perspective, you can provide better service and defuse difficult situations.

Problem-solving skills: Volunteering can help you develop your problem-solving skills, as you may encounter unexpected challenges and have to find creative solutions. This can be particularly helpful in customer service, where you may need to think on your feet to resolve customer issues.

Patience and resilience: Volunteering can also help you develop greater patience and resilience. This can be valuable in customer service, where you may encounter difficult customers or have to handle challenging situations. By remaining calm and patient, you can provide better service and help diffuse difficult situations.

Teamwork and collaboration: Volunteering often involves working in teams to achieve a common goal. This can help you develop your teamwork and collaboration skills, which can be helpful in customer service. By working effectively with your colleagues, you can provide better service and resolve customer issues more efficiently.

Overall, engaging in volunteer service work can provide a range of experiences and skills that can improve your customer service abilities. By developing your communication skills, empathy, problem-solving abilities, patience, resilience, and teamwork skills, you can become a more effective and valuable customer service professional.

Questionnaire

Work Hard

a. How do you define "working hard" in the context of our team?

b. Can you give an example of a time when you went above and beyond to complete a task?

c. How do you prioritize your workload when you have multiple tasks to complete?

d. What motivates you to work hard?

Play by the Rules

a. How do you ensure that you are following our company's rules and policies?

b. How would you handle a situation where you observed a colleague breaking a company rule?

c. How do you define ethical behavior?

d. Can you provide an example of a time when you upheld ethical principles in the workplace?

Innovate

a. How do you approach problem-solving and brainstorming new ideas?

b. What steps do you take to stay current with industry trends and developments?

c. Can you give an example of a time when you introduced a new idea or process that positively impacted the team or company?

d. How do you encourage creativity and innovation in your team members?

Treat People with Respect

a. How do you ensure that you are treating all team members with respect?

b. How do you handle conflicts or disagreements with team members?

c. What steps do you take to promote a diverse and inclusive work environment?

d. How do you address situations where you observe discriminatory behavior or language?

Communicate

a. How do you approach communicating with team members and superiors?

b. How do you ensure that communication is effective and understood by all parties involved?

c. What methods do you use to provide feedback to team members?

d. How do you handle situations where communication breakdowns occur?

Serve

a. How do you define "service" in the context of our company?

b. Can you give an example of a time when you volunteered or provided service to a cause or organization?

c. How do you encourage team members to volunteer or provide service?

d. What steps do you take to ensure that our company is making a positive impact in the community?